AT YOUR COMMAND

D0071531

THE TARCHER CORNERSTONE EDITIONS

Tao Te Ching
by Lao Tzu, translated by Jonathan Star

The Essential Marcus Aurelius
Newly translated and introduced
by Jacob Needleman and John P. Piazza

Accept This Gift: Selections from A Course in Miracles
Edited by Frances Vaughan, Ph.D.,
and Roger Walsh, M.D., Ph.D.

The Kybalion
by Three Initiates

The Spiritual Emerson
Essential Works by Ralph Waldo Emerson
Introduction by Jacob Needleman

The Four Gospels
The Contemporary English Version

The Hermetica: The Lost Wisdom of the Pharaohs
by Timothy Freke and Peter Gandy

Rumi: In the Arms of the Beloved
Translations by Jonathan Star

The Aquarian Gospel of Jesus the Christ
by Levi H. Dowling

The Upanishads: A New Translation
by Vernon Katz and Thomas Egenes

Seven Years in Tibet
by Heinrich Harrer

The Aquarian Conspiracy
by Marilyn Ferguson

The New Religions
by Jacob Needleman

Love's Voice: 72 Kabbalistic Haiku
by Richard Zimler

The Power of Awareness
by Neville

At Your Command
by Neville

The Essential Nostradamus
by Richard Smoley

Bulfinch's Mythology
by Thomas Bulfinch

The Book of the Damned
by Charles Fort

The Ramayana
a new retelling by Linda Egenes and Kumuda Reddy

The Outsider
by Colin Wilson

AT YOUR COMMAND

Neville Goddard

A TarcherPerigee Book

tarcherperigee

An imprint of Penguin Random House LLC
375 Hudson Street
New York, New York 10014

At Your Command was originally published in 1939.

Most TarcherPerigee books are available at special quantity discounts for
bulk purchase for sales promotions, premiums, fund-raising, and educational
needs. Special books or book excerpts also can be created to fit specific
needs. For details, write: SpecialMarkets@penguinrandomhouse.com.

ISBN 9780143129288

Printed in the United States of America

ScoutAutomatedPrintCode

Contents

Letter From Neville

This book contains the very essence of the Principle of Expression. Had I cared to, I could have expanded it into a book of several hundred pages but such expansion would have defeated the purpose of this book.

Commands to be effective—must be short and to the point: the greatest command ever recorded is found in the few simple words, "And God said, 'Let there be light.'"

In keeping with this principle I now give to you, the reader, in these few pages, the truth as it was revealed to me.

NEVILLE

At Your Command

Can man decree a thing and have it come to pass? Most decidedly he can! Man has always decreed that which has appeared in his world and is today decreeing that which is appearing in his world and shall continue to do so as long as man is conscious of being man. Not one thing has ever appeared in man's world but what man decreed that it should. This you may deny, but try as you will you cannot disprove it, for this decreeing is based upon a changeless principle. You do not command things to appear by your words or loud affirmations. Such vain repetition is more often than not confirmation of the opposite. Decreeing is ever done in consciousness. That is; every man is conscious of being that which he has decreed himself to be. The dumb man without using words is conscious of being dumb. Therefore he is decreeing himself to be dumb.

When the Bible is read in this light you will find it to be the greatest scientific book ever written. Instead of looking upon the Bible as the historical record of an ancient civilization or the biography of the unusual life of Jesus, see it as a great psychological drama taking place in the consciousness of man.

Claim it as your own and you will suddenly transform your world from the barren deserts of Egypt to the promised land of Canaan.

Every one will agree with the statement that all things were made by God, and without him there is nothing made that is made, but what man does not agree upon is the identity of God. All the churches and priesthoods of the world disagree as to the identity and true nature of God. The Bible proves beyond the shadow of a doubt that Moses and the prophets were in one hundred per cent accord as to the identity and nature of God. And Jesus' life and teachings are in agreement with the findings of the prophets of old. Moses discovered God to be man's awareness of being, when he declared these little understood words, "I AM hath sent me unto you." David sang in his psalms, "Be still and know that I AM God." Isaiah declared, "I AM the Lord and there is none else. There is no God beside me. I girded thee, though thou hast not known me. I form the light, and create darkness; I make peace, and create evil. I the Lord do all these things."

The *awareness of being* as God is stated hundreds of times in the New Testament. To name but a few: "I AM the shepherd, I AM the door; I AM the resurrection and the life; I AM the way; I AM the Alpha and Omega; I AM the beginning and the end"; and again, "Whom do you say that I AM?"

It is not stated, "I, Jesus, am the door. I, Jesus am the way," nor is it said, "Whom do you say that I, Jesus, am?" It is clearly stated, "I AM the way." The awareness of being is the door through which the manifestations of life pass into the world of form.

Consciousness is the resurrecting power—resurrecting that which man is conscious of being. Man is ever out-picturing that which he is conscious of being. This is the truth that makes man free, for man is always self-imprisoned or self-freed.

If you, the reader, will give up all of your former beliefs in a God apart from yourself, and claim God as your awareness of being—as Jesus and the prophets did— you will transform your world with the realization that, "I and my father are one." This statement, "I and my father are one, but my father is greater than I," seems very confusing—but if interpreted in the light of what we have just said concerning the identity of God, you will find it very revealing. Consciousness, being God, is as 'father.' The thing that you are conscious of being is the 'son' bearing witness of his 'father.' It is like the conceiver and its conceptions. The conceiver is ever greater than his conceptions yet ever remains one with his conception. For instance; before you are conscious of being man, you are first conscious of being.

Then you become conscious of being man. Yet you remain as conceiver, greater than your conception—man.

Jesus discovered this glorious truth and declared himself to be one with God—not a God that man had fashioned. For he never recognized such a God. He said, "If any man should ever come, saying, 'Look here or look there,' believe them not, for the kingdom of God is within you." Heaven is within you. Therefore, when it is recorded that "He went unto his father," it is telling you that he rose in consciousness to the point where he was just conscious of being, thus transcending the limitations of his present conception of himself, called 'Jesus.'

In the awareness of being all things

are possible, he said, "You shall decree a thing and it shall come to pass." This is his decreeing—rising in consciousness to the naturalness of being the thing desired. As he expressed it, "And I, if I be lifted up, I shall draw all men unto me." If I be lifted up in consciousness to the naturalness of the thing desired I will draw the manifestation of that desire unto me. For he states, "No man comes unto me save the father within me draws him, and I and my father are one." Therefore, consciousness is the father that is drawing the manifestations of life unto you.

You are, at this very moment, drawing into your world that which you are now conscious of being. Now you can see what is meant by, "You must be born again."

If you are dissatisfied with your present expression in life the only way to change it, is to take your attention away from that which seems so real to you and rise in consciousness to that which you desire to be. You cannot serve two masters, therefore to take your attention from one state of consciousness and place it upon another is to die to one and live to the other.

The question, "Whom do you say that I AM?" is not addressed to a man called 'Peter' by one called 'Jesus.' This is the eternal question addressed to one's self by one's true being. In other words, "Whom do you say that you are?" For your conviction of yourself—your opinion of yourself will determine your expression in life. He states,

"You believe in God—believe also in me." In other words, it is the me within you that is this God.

Praying then, is seen to be recognizing yourself to be that which you now desire, rather than its accepting form of petitioning a God that does not exist for that which you now desire.

So can't you see why the millions of prayers are unanswered? Men pray to a God that does not exist. For instance: To be conscious of being poor and to pray to a God for riches is to be rewarded with that which you are conscious of being—which is poverty. Prayers to be successful must be claiming rather than begging—so if you would pray for riches turn from your picture of poverty by denying the very evidence of your senses and assume the nature of being wealthy.

We are told, "When you pray go within in secret and shut the door. And that which your father sees in secret, with that will he reward you openly." We have identified the 'father' to be the awareness of being. We have also identified the 'door' to be the awareness of being. So 'shutting the door' is shutting out that which 'I' am now aware of being and claiming myself to be that which 'I' desire to be. The very moment my claim is established to the point of conviction, that moment I begin to draw unto myself the evidence of my claim.

Do not question the how of these things

appearing, for no man knows that way. That is, no manifestation knows how the things desired will appear.

Consciousness is the way or door through which things appear. He said, "I AM the way"—not 'I,' John Smith, am the way, but "I AM," the awareness of being, is the way through which the thing shall come. The signs always follow. They never precede. Things have no reality other than in consciousness. Therefore, get the consciousness first and the thing is compelled to appear.

You are told, "Seek ye first the kingdom of Heaven and all things shall be added unto you." Get first the consciousness of the things that you are seeking and leave the things alone. This is what is meant by "Ye shall decree a thing and it shall come to pass."

Apply this principle and you will know what it is to 'prove me and see.' The story of Mary is the story of every man. Mary was not a woman—giving birth in some miraculous way to one called 'Jesus.' Mary is the awareness of being that ever remains virgin, no matter how many desires it gives birth to. Right now look upon yourself as this virgin Mary—being impregnated by yourself through the medium of desire— becoming one with your desire to the point of embodying or giving birth to your desire.

For instance: It is said of Mary (whom you now know to be yourself) that she know not a man. Yet she conceived. That is, you, John Smith, have no reason to believe that that which you now desire is possible, but having discovered your awareness of being to be God, you make this awareness your husband and conceive a man child (manifestation) of the Lord, "For thy maker is thine husband; the Lord of hosts is his name; the Lord God of the whole earth shall he be called." Your ideal or ambition is this conception—the first command to her, which is now to yourself, is "Go, tell no man." That is, do not discuss your ambitions or desires with another for the other will only echo your present fears. Secrecy is the first law to be observed in realizing your desire.

The second, as we are told in the story of Mary, is to "magnify the Lord." We have identified the Lord as your awareness of being. Therefore, to 'magnify the Lord' is to revalue or expand one's present conception of one's self to the point where this revaluation becomes natural. When this naturalness is attained you give birth by becoming that which you are one with in consciousness.

The story of creation is given us in digest form in the first chapter of John.

"In the beginning was the word." Now, this very second, is the 'beginning' spoken of: It is the beginning of an urge—a desire. 'The word' is the desire swimming around in your consciousness—seeking embodiment. The urge of itself has no reality, for,

"I AM" or the awareness of being is the only reality. Things live only as long as I AM aware of being them; so to realize one's desire, the second line of this first verse of John must be applied. That is, "And the word was with God." The word, or desire, must be fixed or united with consciousness to give it reality. The awareness becomes aware of being the thing desired, thereby nailing itself upon the form or conception—and giving life unto its conception—or resurrecting that which was heretofore a dead or unfulfilled desire. "Two shall agree as touching anything and it shall be established on earth."

This agreement is never made between two persons. It is between the awareness and the thing desired. You are now conscious of being, so you are actually saying to yourself, without using words, "I AM." Now, if it is a state of health that you are desirous of attaining, before you have any evidence of health in your world, you begin to FEEL yourself to be healthy. And the very second the feeling "I AM healthy" is attained the two have agreed. That is, I AM and health have agreed to be one and this agreement ever results in the birth of a child which is the thing agreed upon—in this case, health. And because I made the agreement I express the thing agreed. So you can see why Moses stated, "I AM hath sent me." For what being, other than I AM could send you into expression? None—for

"I AM the way—Beside me there is no other." If you take the wings of the morning and fly into the uttermost parts of the world or if you make your bed in Hell, you will still be aware of being. You are ever sent into expression by your awareness and your expression is ever that which you are aware of being.

Again, Moses stated, "I AM that I AM." Now here is something to always bear in mind. You cannot put new wine in old bottles or new patches upon old garments. That is; you cannot take with you into the new consciousness any part of the old man. All of your present beliefs, fears and limitations are weights that bind you to your present level of consciousness. If you would transcend this level you must leave behind all that is now your present self, or conception of yourself. To do this you take your attention away from all that is now your problem or limitation and dwell upon just being. That is; you say silently but feeling to yourself, "I AM." Do not condition this 'awareness' as yet. Just declare yourself to be, and continue to do so, until you are lost in the feeling of just being—faceless and formless. When this expansion of consciousness is attained, then, within this formless deep of yourself give form to the new conception by FEELING yourself to be THAT which you desire to be.

You will find within this deep of yourself all things to be divinely possible. Everything in the world which you can conceive of being, is to you, within this present formless awareness, a most natural attainment.

The invitation given us in the Scriptures is—"to be absent from the body and be present with the Lord." The 'body' being your former conception of yourself and 'the Lord'—your awareness of being. This is what is meant when Jesus said to Nicodemus, "Ye must be born again for except ye be born again ye cannot enter the kingdom of Heaven." That is; except you leave behind you your present conception of yourself and assume the nature of the new birth, you will continue to out-picture your present limitations.

The only way to change your expressions

of life is to change your consciousness. For consciousness is the reality that eternally solidifies itself in the things round about you. Man's world in its every detail is his consciousness out-pictured. You can no more change your environment, or world, by destroying things than you can your reflection by destroying the mirror. Your environment, and all within it, reflects that which you are in consciousness. As long as you continue to be that in consciousness so long will you continue to out-picture it in your world.

Knowing this, begin to revalue yourself. Man has placed too little value upon himself. In the Book of Numbers you will read, "In that day there were giants in the land; and we were in our own sight as grasshoppers. And we were in their sight as grasshoppers." This does not mean a time in the dim past when man had the stature of giants. Today is the day—the eternal now—when conditions round about you have attained the appearance of giants (such as unemployed, the armies of your enemy, your problems and all things that seem to threaten you) those are the giant that make you feel yourself to be a grasshopper. But, you are told, you were first, in your own sight a grasshopper and because of this you were to the giants—a grasshopper. In other words, you can only be to others what you are first to yourself. Therefore, to revalue yourself and begin to feel yourself to be the giant, a center of power, is to dwarf these former giants and make of them grasshoppers. "All the inhabitants of the earth are as nothing, and he doeth according to his will in the armies of Heaven and among all the inhabitants of the earth; and none can stay his hand, nor say unto him, 'What doest thou?'" This being spoken of is not the orthodox God sitting in space but the one and only God—the everlasting father, your awareness of being. So awake to the power that you are, not as man, but as your true self, a faceless, formless awareness, and free yourself from your self imposed prison.

"I am the good shepherd and know my sheep and am known of mine. My sheep hear my voice and I know them and they will follow me." Awareness is the good shepherd. What I am aware of being, is the 'sheep' that follow me. So good a 'shepherd' is your awareness that it has never lost one of the 'sheep' that you are aware of being.

I am a voice calling in the wilderness of human confusion for such as I am aware of being, and never shall there come a time when that which I am convinced that I am shall fail to find me. "I AM" is an open door for all that I am to enter. Your awareness of being is lord and shepherd of your life. So, "The Lord is my shepherd; I shall not want" is seen in its true light now to be your consciousness. You could never be in want of proof or lack the evidence of that which you are aware of being.

This being true, why not become aware of being great; God-loving; wealthy; healthy; and all attributes that you admire?

It is just as easy to possess the consciousness of these qualities as it is to possess their opposites for you have not your present consciousness because of your world. On the contrary, your world is what it is because of your present consciousness. Simple, is it not? Too simple in fact for the wisdom of man that tries to complicate everything.

Paul said of this principle, "It is to the Greeks" (or wisdom of this world) "foolishness." "And to the Jews" (or those who look for signs) "a stumbling block"; with the result, that man continues to walk in darkness rather than awake to the being that he is. Man has so long worshipped the images of his own making that at first he finds this revelation blasphemous, since it spells death to all his previous beliefs in a God apart from himself. This revelation will bring the knowledge that "I and my father are one but my father is greater than I." You are one with your present conception of yourself. But you are greater than that which you are at present aware of being.

Before man can attempt to transform his world he must first lay the foundation—"I AM the Lord." That is, man's awareness, his consciousness of being is God. Until this is firmly established so that no suggestion or argument put forward by others can shake it, he will find himself returning to the slavery of his former beliefs. "If ye believe not that I AM he, ye shall die in your sins." That is, you shall continue to be confused and thwarted until you find the cause of your confusion. When you have lifted up the son of man then shall you know that I AM he, that is, that I, John Smith, do nothing of myself, but my father, or that state of consciousness which I am now one with does the works.

When this is realized every urge and desire that springs within you shall find expression in your world. "Behold I stand at the door and knock. If any man hear my voice and open the door I will come in to him and sup with him and he with me." The "I" knocking at the door is the urge.

The door is your consciousness. To open the door is to become one with that which is knocking by FEELING oneself to be the thing desired. To feel one's desire as impossible is to shut the door or deny this urge expression. To rise in consciousness to the naturalness of the thing felt is to swing wide the door and invite this one into embodiment.

That is why it is constantly recorded that Jesus left the world of manifestation and ascended unto his father. Jesus, as you and I, found all things impossible to Jesus, as man. But having discovered his father to be the state of consciousness of the thing desired, he but left behind him the "Jesus consciousness" and rose in consciousness to that state desired and stood upon it until he became one with it. As he made himself one with that, he became that in expression.

This is Jesus' simple message to man: Men are but garments that the impersonal being, I AM—the presence that men call God—dwells in. Each garment has certain limitations. In order to transcend these limitations and give expression to that which, as man—John Smith—you find yourself incapable of doing, you take your attention away from your present limitations, or John Smith conception of yourself, and merge yourself in the feeling of being that which you desire. Just how this desire or newly attained consciousness will embody itself, no man knows. For I, or the newly attained consciousness, has ways that ye know not of; its ways are past finding out. Do not speculate as to the HOW of this consciousness embodying itself, for no man is wise enough to know the how. Speculation is proof that you have not attained to the naturalness of being the thing desired and so are filled with doubts.

You are told, "He who lacks wisdom let him ask of God, that gives to all liberally, and upbraideth not; and it shall be given unto him. But let him ask not doubting for he who doubts is as a wave of the sea that is tossed and battered by the winds. And let not such a one think that he shall receive anything from the Lord." You can see why this statement is made, for only upon the rock of faith can anything be established. If you have not the consciousness of the thing you have not the cause or foundation upon which the thing is erected.

A proof of this established consciousness is given you in the words, "Thank you, father." When you come into the joy of thanksgiving so that you actually feel grateful for having received that which is not yet apparent to the senses, you have definitely become one in consciousness with the thing for which you gave thanks. God (your awareness) is not mocked. You are ever receiving that which you are aware of being and no man gives thanks for something which he has not received. "Thank you, father" is not, as it is used by many today a sort of magical formula. You need never utter aloud the words, "Thank you, father." In applying this principle as you rise in consciousness to the point where you are really grateful and happy for having received the thing desired, you automatically rejoice and give thanks inwardly. You have already accepted the gift which was but a desire before you rose in consciousness, and your faith is now the substance that shall clothe your desire.

This rising in consciousness is the spiritual marriage where two shall agree upon being one and their likeness or image is established on earth.

"For whatsoever ye ask in my name the same give I unto you." 'Whatsoever' is quite a large measure. It is the unconditional. It does not state if society deems it right or wrong that you should ask it, it rests with you. Do you really want it? Do you desire it? That is all that is necessary. Life will give it to you if you ask 'in his name.'

His name is not a name that you pronounce with the lips. You can ask forever in the name of God or Jehovah or Christ Jesus and you will ask in vain. 'Name' means nature; so, when you ask in the nature of a thing, results ever follow. To ask in the name is to rise in consciousness and become one in nature with the thing desired, rise in consciousness to the nature of the thing, and you will become that thing in expression. Therefore, "what things soever ye desire, when ye pray, believe that ye receive them and ye shall receive them."

Praying, as we have shown you before, is recognition—the injunction to believe that ye receive is first person, present tense. This means that you must be in the nature of the things asked for before you can receive them.

To get into the nature easily, general amnesty is necessary. We are told, "Forgive if ye have aught against any, that your father also, which is in Heaven, may forgive you. But if ye forgive not, neither will your father forgive you." This may seem to be some personal God who is pleased or displeased with your actions but this is not the case.

Consciousness, being God, if you hold in consciousness anything against man, you are binding that condition in your world. But to release man from all condemnation is to free yourself so that you may rise to any level necessary; there is therefore, no condemnation to those in Christ Jesus.

Therefore, a very good practice before you enter into your meditation is first to free every man in the world from blame. For LAW is never violated and you can rest confidently in the knowledge that every man's conception of himself is going to be his reward. So you do not have to bother yourself about seeing whether or not man gets what you consider he should get. For life makes no mistakes and always gives man that which man first gives himself.

This brings us to that much abused statement of the Bible on tithing. Teachers of all kinds have enslaved man with this affair of tithing, for not themselves understanding the nature of tithing and being themselves fearful of lack, they have led their followers to believe that a tenth part of their income should be given to the Lord. Meaning, as they make very clear, that, when one gives a tenth part of his income to their particular organization he is giving his "tenth part" to the Lord—(or is tithing). But remember, "I AM the Lord." Your awareness of being is the God that you give to and you ever give in this manner.

Therefore when you claim yourself to be anything, you have given that claim or quality to God. And your awareness of being, which is no respecter of persons, will return to you pressed down, shaken together, and running over with that quality or attribute which you claim for yourself.

Awareness of being is nothing that you could ever name. To claim God to be rich; to be great; to be love; to be all wise; is to define that which cannot be defined. For God is nothing that could ever be named.

Tithing is necessary and you do tithe with God. But from now on give to the only God and see to it that you give him the quality that you desire as man to express by claiming yourself to be the great, the wealthy, the loving, the all wise.

Do not speculate as to how you shall express these qualities or claims, for life has a way that you, as man, know not of. Its ways are past finding out. But, I assure you, the day you claim these qualities to the point of conviction, your claims will be honored. There is nothing covered that shall not be uncovered. That which is spoken in secret shall be proclaimed from the housetops. That is, your secret convictions of yourself—these secret claims that no man knows of, when really believed, will be shouted from the housetops in your world. For your convictions of yourself are the words of the God within you, which words are spirit and cannot return unto you void but must accomplish whereunto they are sent.

You are at this moment calling out of the infinite that which you are now conscious of being. And not one word or conviction will fail to find you.

"I AM the vine and ye are the branches." Consciousness is the 'vine,' and those qualities which you are now conscious of being are as 'branches' that you feed and keep alive. Just as a branch has no life except it be rooted in the vine, so likewise things have no life except you be conscious of them. Just as a branch withers and dies if the sap of the vine ceases to flow towards it, so do things in your world pass away if you take your attention from them, because your attention is as the sap of life that keeps alive and sustains the things of your world.

To dissolve a problem that now seems so real to you all that you do is remove your attention from it. In spite of its seeming reality, turn from it in consciousness. Become indifferent and begin to feel yourself to be that which would be the solution of the problem.

For instance; if you were imprisoned no man would have to tell you that you should desire freedom. Freedom, or rather the desire of freedom would be automatic. So why look behind the four walls of your prison bars? Take your attention from being imprisoned and begin to feel yourself to be free. FEEL it to the point where it is natural—the very second you do so, those prison bars will dissolve. Apply this same principle to any problem.

I have seen people who were in debt up to their ears apply this principle and in the twinkling of an eye debts that were mountainous were removed. I have seen those whom doctors had given up as incurable take their attention away from their problem of disease and begin to feel themselves to be well in spite of the evidence of their sense to the contrary. In no time at all this so called 'incurable disease' vanished and left no scar.

Your answer to, "Whom do you say that I AM?" ever determines your expression.

As long as you are conscious of being imprisoned or diseased, or poor, so long will you continue to out-picture or express these conditions.

When man realized that he is *now* that which he is seeking and begins to claim that he is, he will have the proof of his claim. This cue is given you in words, "Whom seek ye?" And they answered, "Jesus." And the voice said, "I am he." 'Jesus' here means salvation or savior. You are seeking to be salvaged from that which is not your problem.

"I AM" is he that will save you. If you are hungry, your savior is food. If you are poor, your savior is riches. If you are imprisoned, your savior is freedom. If you are diseased, it will not be a man called Jesus who will save you, but health will become your savior. Therefore, claim "I am he," in other words, claim yourself to be the thing desired. Claim it in consciousness—not in words—and consciousness will reward you with your claim. You are told, "You shall find me when you FEEL after me." Well, FEEL after that quality in consciousness until you FEEL yourself to be it. When you lose yourself in the feeling of being it, the quality will embody itself in your world.

You are healed from your problem when you touch the solution of it. "Who has touched me? For I perceive virtue is gone out of me." Yes, the day you touch this being within you—FEELING yourself to be cured or healed, virtues will come out of your very self and solidify themselves in your world as healings.

It is said, "You believe in God. Believe also in me for I am he." Have the faith of God. "He made himself one with God and found it not robbery to do the works of God." Go you and do likewise. Yes, begin to believe your awareness, your consciousness of being to be God. Claim for yourself all the attributes that you have heretofore given an external God and you will begin to express these claims.

"For I am not a God afar off. I am nearer than your hands and feet—nearer than your very breathing." I am your awareness of being. I am that in which all that I shall ever be aware of being shall begin and end. "For before the world was I AM; and when the world shall cease to be, I AM; before Abraham was, I AM." This I AM is your awareness.

"Except the Lord build the house they labor in vain that build it." 'The Lord,' being your consciousness, except that which you seek is first established in your consciousness, you will labor in vain to find it. All things must begin and end in consciousness.

So, blessed indeed is the man that trusteth in himself—for man's faith in God will ever be measured by his confidence in himself. You believe in a God, believe also in ME.

Put not your trust in men for men but reflect the being that you are, and can only bring to you or do unto you that which you have first done unto yourself.

"No man taketh away my life, I lay it down myself." I have the power to lay it down and the power to take it up again.

No matter what happens to man in this world it is never an accident. It occurs under the guidance of an exact and change-less Law.

"No man" (manifestation) "comes unto me except the father within me draw him," and "I and my father are one." Believe this truth and you will be free. Man has always blamed others for that which he is and will continue to do so until he find himself as cause of all. "I AM" comes not to destroy but to fulfill.

"I AM," the awareness within you, destroys nothing but ever fills full the molds or conception one has of one's self.

It is impossible for the poor man to find wealth in this world no matter how he is surrounded with it until he first claims himself to be wealthy. For signs follow, they do not precede. To constantly kick and complain against the limitations of poverty while remaining poor in consciousness is to play the fool's game. Changes cannot take place from that level of consciousness for life is constantly out-picturing all levels.

Follow the example of the prodigal son. Realize that you, yourself brought about this condition of waste and lack and make the decision within yourself to rise to a higher level where the fatted calf, the ring, and the robe await your claim.

There was no condemnation of the prodigal when he had the courage to claim this inheritance as his own. Others will condemn us only as long as we continue in that for which we condemn ourselves. So: "Happy is the man that condemneth himself not in that which he alloweth." For to life nothing is condemned. All is expressed.

Life does not care whether you call yourself rich or poor; strong or weak. It will eternally reward you with that which you claim as true of yourself.

The measurements of right and wrong belong to man alone. To life there is nothing right or wrong. As Paul stated in his letters to the Romans: "I know and am persuaded by the Lord Jesus that there is nothing unclean of itself, but to him that esteemeth anything to be unclean, to him it is unclean." Stop asking yourself whether you are worthy or unworthy to receive that which you desire. You, as man, did not create the desire. Your desires are ever fashioned within you because of what you now claim yourself to be.

When a man is hungry (without thinking), he automatically desires food. When imprisoned, he automatically desires freedom and so forth. Your desires contain within themselves the plan of self-expression.

So leave all judgments out of the picture

and rise in consciousness to the level of your desire and make yourself one with it by claiming it to be so now. For: "My grace is sufficient for thee. My strength is made perfect in weakness."

Have faith in this unseen claim until the conviction is born within you that it is so. Your confidence in this claim will pay great rewards. Just a little while and he, the thing desired, will come. But without faith it is impossible to realize anything. Through faith the worlds were framed because "faith is the substance of the thing hoped for—the evidence of the thing not yet seen."

Don't be anxious or concerned as to results. They will follow just as surely as day follows night.

Look upon your desires—all of them—
as the spoken words of God, and every word
or desire a promise. The reason most of us
fail to realize our desires is because we are
constantly conditioning them. Do not condition your desire. Just accept it as it comes
to you. Give thanks for it to the point that
you are grateful for having already received
it—then go about your way in peace.

Such acceptance of your desire is like
dropping seed—fertile seed—into prepared
soil. For when you can drop the thing
desired in consciousness, confident that
it shall appear, you have done all that is
expected to you. But, to be worried or
concerned about the HOW of your desire
maturing is to hold these fertile seeds in a

mental grasp, and, therefore, never to have dropped them in the soil of confidence.

The reason men condition their desires is because they constantly judge after the appearance of being and see the things as real—forgetting that the only reality is the consciousness back of them.

To see things as real is to deny that all things are possible to God. The man who is imprisoned and sees his four walls as real is automatically denying the urge or promise of God within him of freedom.

A question often asked when this statement is made is: If one's desire is a gift of God how can you say that if one desires to kill a man that such a desire is good and therefore God sent? In answer to this, let me say that no man desires to kill another. What he does desire is to be freed from such a one. But because he does not believe that the desire to be free from such a one contains within itself the powers of freedom, he conditions that desire and sees the only way to express such freedom is to destroy the man—forgetting that the life wrapped within the desire has ways that he, as man, knows not of. Its ways are past finding out. Thus man distorts the gifts of God through his lack of faith.

Problems are the mountains spoken of that can be removed if one has but the faith of a grain of a mustard seed. Men approach their problem as did the old lady who, on attending service and hearing the priest say, "If you had but the faith of a grain of a mustard seed you would say unto yonder mountain 'be thou removed' and it shall be removed and nothing is impossible to you."

That night as she said her prayers, she quoted this part of the scriptures and retired to bed in what she thought was faith. On arising in the morning she rushed to the window and exclaimed: "I knew that old mountain would still be there."

For this is how man approaches his problem. He knows that they are still going to confront him. And because life is no respecter of persons and destroys nothing, it continues to keep alive that which he is conscious of being.

Things will disappear only as man

changes in consciousness. Deny it if you will, it still remains a fact that consciousness is the only reality and things but mirror that which you are in consciousness. So the heavenly state you are seeking will be found only in consciousness, for the kingdom of heaven is within you. As the will of heaven is ever done on earth you are today living in the heaven that you have established within you. For here on this very earth your heaven reveals itself. The kingdom of heaven really is at hand. NOW is the accepted time. So create a new heaven, enter into a new state of consciousness and a new earth will appear.

"The former things shall pass away. They shall not be remembered nor come into

mind any more. For behold, I" (your consciousness) "come quickly and my reward is
with me."

I am nameless but will take upon myself
every name (nature) that you call me.
Remember it is you, yourself, that I speak
of as 'me.' So every conception that you
have of yourself—that is, every deep conviction—you have of yourself is that which
you shall appear as being—for I AM not
fooled; God is not mocked.

Now let me instruct you in the art of
fishing. It is recorded that the disciples
fished all night and caught nothing. Then
Jesus came upon the scene and told them to
cast their nets in once more, into the same
waters that only a moment before were

barren—and this time their nets were bursting with the catch.

This story is taking place in the world today right within you, the reader. For you have within you all the elements necessary to go fishing. But until you find that Jesus Christ (your awareness) is Lord, you will fish, as did these disciples, in the night of human darkness. That is, you will fish for THINGS thinking things to be real and will fish with the human bait—which is a struggle and an effort—trying to make contact with this one and that one: trying to coerce this being or the other being; and all such effort will be in vain. But when you discover your awareness of being to be Christ Jesus you will let him direct your fishing. And you will fish in consciousness for the things that you desire. For your desire—will be the fish that you will catch, because your consciousness is the only living reality you will fish in the deep waters of consciousness.

If you would catch that which is beyond your present capacity you must launch out into deeper waters, for, within your present consciousness such fish or desires cannot swim. To launch out into deeper waters, you leave behind you all that is now your present problem, or limitation, by taking your ATTENTION AWAY from it. Turn your back completely upon every problem and limitation that you now possess.

Dwell upon just being by saying, "I

AM," "I AM," "I AM," to yourself. Continue to declare to yourself that you just are. Do not condition this declaration, just continue to FEEL yourself to be and without warning you will find yourself slipping the anchor that tied you to the shallow of your problems and moving out into the deep.

This is usually accompanied with the feeling of expansion. You will FEEL yourself expand as though you were actually growing. Don't be afraid, for courage is necessary. You are not going to die to anything by your former limitations, but they are going to die as you move away from them, for they live only in your consciousness. In this deep or expanded consciousness you will find yourself to be a power that you had never dreamt of before.

The things desired before you shoved off from the shores of limitation are the fish you are going to catch in this deep. Because you have lost all consciousness of your problems and barriers, it is now the easiest thing in the world to FEEL yourself to be one with the things desired.

Because I AM (your consciousness) is the resurrection and the life, you must attach this resurrecting power that you are to the thing desired if you would make it appear and live in your world. Now you begin to assume the nature of the thing desired by feeling, "I AM wealthy"; "I AM free"; "I AM strong." When these 'FEELS' are fixed within yourself, your formless being will take upon itself the forms of the things felt. You become 'crucified' upon the feelings of wealth, freedom, and strength.—Remain buried in the stillness of these convictions. Then, as a thief in the night and when you least expect it, these qualities will be resurrected in your world as living realities.

The world shall touch you and see that you are flesh and blood for you shall begin to bear fruit of the nature of these qualities newly appropriated. This is the art of successful fishing for the manifestations of life.

Successful realization of the thing desired is also told us in the story of Daniel in the lion's den. Here, it is recorded that Daniel, while in the lion's den, turned his back upon the lions and looked towards the light coming from above; that the lions remained powerless and Daniel's faith in his God saved him.

This also is your story and you too must do as Daniel did. If you found yourself in a lion's den you would have no other concern but lions. You would not be thinking of one thing in the world but your problem—which problem would be lions.

Yet, you are told that Daniel turned his back upon them and looked towards the light that was his God. If we would follow the example of Daniel we would, while imprisoned within the den of poverty of sickness, take our attention away from our problems of debts or sickness and dwell upon the thing we seek.

If we do not look back in consciousness to our problems but continue in faith—believing ourselves to be that which we seek, we too will find our prison walls open and the thing sought—yes, "whatsoever things"—realized.

Another story is told us; of the widow and the three drops of oil. The prophet asked the widow, "What have ye in your house?" And she replied, "Three drops of oil." He then said to her, "Go borrow vessels. Close the door after ye have returned into your house and begin to pour." And she poured from three drops of oil into all the borrowed vessels, filling them to capacity with oil remaining.

You, the reader, are this widow. You have not a husband to impregnate you or make you fruitful, for a 'widow' is a barren state. Your awareness is now the Lord—or the prophet that has become your husband.

Follow the example of the widow, who instead of recognizing an emptiness or nothingness, recognized the something— three drops of oil.

Then the command to her, "Go within and close the door," that is, shut the door of the senses that tell you of the empty measures, the debts, the problems.

When you have taken your attention

away completely by shutting out the evidence of the senses, begin to FEEL the joy—
(symbolized by oil)—of having received
the things desired. When the agreement is
established within you so that all doubts and
fears have passed away, then, you too will fill
all the empty measures of your life and will
have an abundance running over.

Recognition is the power that con-
jures in the world. Every state that you
have ever recognized, you have embodied.
That which you are recognizing as true of
yourself today is that which you are experi-
encing. So be as the widow and recognize
joy, no matter how little the beginnings of
recognition, and you will be generously
rewarded—for the world is a magnified

mirror, magnifying everything that you are conscious of being.

"I AM the Lord the God, which has brought thee out of the land of Egypt, out of the house of bondage; thou shalt have no other gods before me." What a glorious revelation, your awareness now revealed as the Lord thy God! Come, awake from your dream of being imprisoned. Realize that the earth is yours, "and the fullness thereof; the world, and all that dwells therein."

You have become so enmeshed in the belief that you are man that you have forgotten the glorious being that you are. Now with your memory restored DECREE the unseen to appear and it

SHALL appear, for all things are compelled to respond to the Voice of God, your awareness of being—the world is AT YOUR COMMAND!

Neville Goddard

A Cosmic Philosopher

BY MITCH HOROWITZ

The words of spiritual writer and lecturer Neville Goddard retain their power to electrify more than forty years after his death. In a sonorous, clipped tone that was preserved on thousands of tape recordings made during his lifetime, and now widely circulated online, Neville asserted with complete ease what many would find fantastical: The human imagination is God—and our thoughts create our world, in the most literal sense.

Neville Goddard was perhaps the last century's most intellectually substantive and charismatic purveyor of the philosophy generally called New Thought. He wrote more than ten books under the solitary pen name Neville and was a popular speaker on metaphysical themes from the late 1930s until his death in 1972.

Possessed of a self-educated and uncommonly sharp intellect, Neville espoused a spiritual vision that was bold and total: Everything you see and experience, including other people, is the result of your own thoughts and emotional states. Each of us dreams into existence an infinitude of realities and outcomes. When you realize this, Neville taught, you will discover yourself to be a slumbering branch of the Creator clothed in human form, and at the helm of limitless possibilities.

Neville's thought system influenced a wide range of spiritual thinkers and writers, from bestselling author Joseph Murphy to mystical iconoclast Carlos Castaneda. He now has an ardent online following, connected by the proliferation of his digitized lectures and books. More still, Neville's reputation is growing as his mystical teachings are found to comport with key issues in today's quantum physics debate.

Yet little is known about this spiritual teacher who exerted so unusual a pull on the American spiritual scene of the latter twentieth century. Neville cultivated an air of mystery, which has contributed to the intrigue and questions around his ideas—and where they came from.

A PHILOSOPHER
BORN

Neville Lancelot Goddard was born on February 19, 1905, on the then British-protectorate of Barbados in the town of St. Michael to an Anglican family of nine sons and one daughter. A 1950s gossip column described the young Neville as "enormously wealthy," his family possessing "a whole island in the West Indies."

The truth was far more modest. Neville depicted his own English childhood home as happy but threadbare. There was constant jostling among his brothers for clothes and second helpings at the dinner table. Neville came to New York City at the age of seventeen to study theater—a move that led to a successful career as a vaudeville dancer and Broadway actor. He toured America and England with dance troupes. But Neville's theater life was hand-to-mouth; he supplemented his income by working as an elevator operator and shipping clerk.

The young performer's ambition for the stage began to fade as he encountered an alluring range of spiritual ideas—first with self-styled occult groups and later with the help of a life-transforming mentor. In his lectures, Neville described studying with a turbaned, Ethiopian-born rabbi named

Abdullah. Their initial meeting, Neville said, had an air of kismet:

> When I first met my friend Abdullah back in 1931 I entered a room where he was speaking and when the speech was ended he came over, extended his hand, and said: "Neville, you are six months late." I had never seen the man before, so I said: "I am six months late? How do you know me?" And he replied: "The brothers told me that you were coming and you are six months late."

According to Neville, the two studied Hebrew, Scripture, and Kabbalah together for five years—planting the seeds of Neville's philosophy of mental creativity.

Neville said that his first understanding of the power of creative thought came while he was living in a rented room on Manhattan's Upper West Side during the winter of 1933. The young man was depressed: his theatrical career had stalled and his pockets were empty. "After twelve years in America, I was a failure in my own eyes," he later said. "I was in the theater and made money one year and spent it the next month." The twenty-eight-year-old ached to spend Christmas with his family in Barbados; but he couldn't afford to travel.

"Live as though you are there," Abdullah told him, "and that you shall be."

Wandering the streets of New York City, Neville *thought from his aim*—as he would later urge his listeners—and adopted the feeling that he was really and truly at home on his native island. "Abdullah taught me the importance of remaining faithful to an idea and not compromising," he recalled. "I wavered, but he remained faithful to the assumption that I was in Barbados and had traveled first class."

One December morning before the last ship was to depart New York that year for Barbados, Neville received a letter from a long out-of-touch brother: In it was $50 and a ticket to sail. His experiment, it seemed, had worked.

Neville discovered what eventually

became the hallmark of his philosophy: It is imperative to assume the *feeling* that one's goal has already been attained. "It is not what you want that you attract," he wrote. "You attract what you believe to be true."

FEELING IS
THE SECRET

Neville grew convinced that Scripture was rife with this idea that man had to *think from the end*. He called it the state of 'I AM'— this being a mystical translation of the name of God. Man could attain any goal, he reasoned, provided he adopted *the feeling of it in the present*. Neville reinterpreted each episode in Scripture as a psychological parable of this truth. In an example from his 1941 book *Your Faith Is Your Fortune* he took a fresh sounding of the tale of Lot's wife, who turns into a pillar of salt after looking back upon the city of Sodom: "Not knowing that consciousness is ever out-picturing itself in conditions round about you, like Lot's wife you continually look back upon your problem and again become hypnotized by its seeming naturalness."

In his eyes, all of Scripture was nothing other than a blueprint for man's development. "The Bible has no reference at all to any person who ever existed, or any event that ever occurred upon earth," Neville told audiences. "All the stories of the Bible unfold in the minds of the individual man." Neville depicted Christ not as a living figure but, rather, as a mythical master psychologist whose miracles and parables demonstrate the power of creative thought.

REAL MAGIC

In public talks, Neville often made extravagant claims—such as his use of mental visualizations to win an honorable discharge from the U.S. Army after being drafted at the height of World War II. In actuality, such a sudden discharge did occur.

Neville entered the army on November 12, 1942, obligated to serve for the duration of the war. But military records show that four months later, in March 1943, the mystic was "discharged from service to accept employment in an essential wartime industry."

Neville resumed his "essential wartime"

job as a metaphysical lecturer in New York's Greenwich Village. A profile in *The New Yorker* of September 11, 1943, described the handsome speaker back at the lectern before swooning (and often female) New York audiences.

It is unclear why Neville, a lithe man in perfect health, would have been released from the military at the peak of the war. "Unfortunately," an army public affairs officer said, "Mr. Goddard's records were destroyed in the 1973 fire at the National Personnel Records Center."

Neville also made bold claims about the eventual—and highly prosperous—rise of his family's food service and retail businesses in Barbados. These claims likewise conform to public records.

Even Neville's tales about the mysterious teacher Abdullah are far from dismissible.

HIDDEN MASTERS

Neville's description of training under a turbaned spiritual adept had a certain pedigree in America's alternative spiritual culture. It was a concept that the Russian mystic Madame H. P. Blavatsky ignited in the minds of Western seekers with her late nineteenth-century accounts of her mentorship to unseen *Mahatmas*, or Great Souls. Blavatsky aroused a hope that invisible help was out there; that guidance could be sought from a difficult-to-place master of wisdom, someone who might arrive from an exotic land, or another plane of existence, and who could dispense illumined knowledge.

Indeed, the Abdullah story as told by Neville might be brushed aside as a tale borrowed and retouched from Blavatsky—except for another, better-known figure in the positive-thinking tradition who, toward the end of his life, made his own claims of mentorship under Abdullah.

The Irish emigrant writer Joseph Murphy arrived in New York City in the early 1920s with a degree in chemistry and a passion to study metaphysics. Murphy is widely remembered for his 1963 megaseller *The Power of Your Subconscious Mind*. The book remains one of the most engaging and popular works of positive-mind metaphysics. Shortly before his death in 1981, Murphy, in a little-known series of interviews published by a French press in Quebec, described his own encounter with the mysterious Abdullah. Interviewer Bernard Cantin recounted the tale in his 1987 book of dialogues with Murphy:

> It was in New York that Joseph Murphy also met the professor Abdullah, a Jewish man of black ancestry, a native of Israel, who knew, in every detail, all the symbolism of each of the verses of the Old and the New Testaments. This meeting was one of the most significant in Dr. Murphy's spiritual evolution. In fact, Abdullah, who had never seen nor known the Murphy family, said flatly that Murphy came

from a family of six children, and not five, as Murphy himself had believed. Later on, Murphy, intrigued, questioned his mother and learned that, indeed, he had had another brother who had died a few hours after his birth, and was never spoken of again.

By the mid-1950s Neville's story of tutelage under a secretive teacher exerted a pull on a budding writer whose own memoirs of mystic discovery later made him a near-household name: Carlos Castaneda.

Castaneda wove his own tales of mentorship to a shadowy instructor, in his case a Native American sorcerer named Don Juan. Castaneda first discovered

Neville through an early love interest in Los Angeles, Margaret Runyon, who was among Neville's most dedicated students. A cousin of American storyteller Damon Runyon, Margaret wooed the Latin art student at a friend's house, slipping Carlos a slender Neville volume called *The Search,* in which she had inscribed her name and phone number. The two became lovers and later husband and wife.

Runyon spoke frequently to Castaneda about her mystical teacher Neville, but he responded with little more than mild interest—with one exception. In her memoirs, Runyon recalled Castaneda growing fascinated when the conversation turned to Neville's discipleship under an exotic teacher:

It was more than the message that attracted Carlos, it was Neville himself. He was so mysterious. Nobody was really sure who he was or where he had come from. There were vague references to Barbados in the West Indies and his being the son of an ultra-rich plantation family, but nobody knew for sure. They couldn't even be sure about this Abdullah business, his Indian teacher, who was always *way back there* in the jungle, or someplace. The only thing you really knew was that Neville was here and that he might be back next week, but then again . . .

"There was," she concluded, "a certain power in that position, an appealing kind of freedom in the lack of past and Carlos knew it."

THE MASTER
REVEALED?

Was there a real esoteric teacher named
Abdullah who taught Neville and Joseph
Murphy? A plausible candidate exists. He
is found in the figure of a 1920s- and '30s-
era black nationalist mystic named Arnold
Josiah Ford. Like Neville, Ford was born in
Barbados, in 1877, the son of an itinerant
preacher. Ford arrived in Harlem around
1910 and established himself as a leading
voice in the Ethiopianism movement, a pre-
cursor to Jamaican Rastafarianism.

Both movements held that the East

African nation of Ethiopia was home to a lost Israelite tribe that had preserved the teachings of a mystical African belief system. Ford considered himself an original Israelite, and a man of authentic Judaic descent. Like Abdullah, Ford was considered an 'Ethiopian rabbi.' Surviving photographs show Ford as a dignified, somewhat severe-looking man with a set jaw and penetrating gaze, wearing a turban, just like Neville's Abdullah. Ford himself cultivated an air of mystery, attracting "much apocryphal and often contradictory speculation," noted Randall K. Burkett, a historian of black nationalist movements.

Ford lived in New York City at the

same time that Neville began his discipleship with Abdullah. Neville recalled his and
Abdullah's first meeting in 1931; and U.S.
Census records show Ford was living in
Harlem on West 131st Street in 1930. (He
was also at the same address in 1920, shortly
before Joseph Murphy arrived.) Historian
Howard Brotz, in a study of the black Jew-
ish movement in Harlem, wrote of Ford: "It
is certain that he studied Hebrew with some
immigrant teacher and was a key link" in
communicating "approximations of Talmu-
dic Judaism" from within the Ethiopianism
movement. This would fit Neville's depic-
tion of Abdullah tutoring him in Hebrew
and Kabbalah. (It should be noted that early
twentieth-century occultists often loosely

used the term *Kabbalah* to denote any kind of Judaic study.)

More still, Ford's philosophy of Ethiopianism possessed a mental metaphysics. "The philosophy," noted historian Jill Watts, "contained an element of mind-power, for many adherents of Ethiopianism subscribed to mental healing and believed that material circumstances could be altered through God's power. Such notions closely paralleled tenets of New Thought." Ford was also an early supporter of black nationalist pioneer Marcus Garvey and served as the musical director of Garvey's Universal Negro Improvement Association. Garvey had also suffused his movement with New Thought metaphysics and phraseology.

The commonalities between Ford and Abdullah are striking: the black rabbi, the turban, the study of Hebrew, mind-power metaphysics, the Barbados connection, and the time frame. All suggest Ford as a viable candidate for the elusive Abdullah.

Yet there are too many gaps in both Neville's and Ford's backgrounds to allow for a conclusive leap. Records of Ford's life grow thinner after 1931, the year he departed New York and migrated to Ethiopia. Ethiopian emperor Haile Selassie, after his coronation in 1930, offered land grants to any African-American willing to relocate to the East African nation. Ford accepted the offer. The timing of Ford's departure is the biggest single blow to the

Abdullah–Ford theory. Neville said that he and his teacher had studied together for five years. This obviously would not have been possible with Ford, who had apparently left New York in 1931, the same year Neville said that he and Abdullah first met.

In a coda to Ford's career, he journeyed to Africa, along with several other American followers of Ethiopianism, to accept the land grants offered by Haile Selassie. Yet Ford's life in the Ethiopian countryside, a period so sadly sparse of records, could only have been a difficult existence for the urbane musician. Here was a man uprooted from metropolitan surroundings at an advanced age to settle into a new and unfamiliar agricultural landscape. All the while, Ethiopia was facing the threat of invasion by fascist Italy. Ford died in Ethiopia in September 1935, a few weeks before Mussolini's troops crossed the border.

While Ford's migration runs counter to Neville's timeline, there are other ways in which Ford may fit into the Abdullah mythos. Neville could have extrapolated Abdullah from Ford's character after spending a briefer time with Ford. Or Abdullah may have been a metaphorical composite of several contemporaneous figures, perhaps including Ford.* Or, finally, Abdullah

---

* Neville may have hinted as much, especially in light of his love for Hebrew symbolism. He affectionately called Abdullah 'Ab' for short—a variant of the Hebrew *abba* for 'father.' Neville may have fashioned a mythical 'father mentor' from various teachers.

may have been Neville's invention, though this scenario doesn't account for Joseph Murphy's record.

The full story may never be knowable, but the notion of two young metaphysical seekers, Neville and Murphy, living in prewar New York and studying under an African-American esoteric teacher, whether Ford or another, is wholly plausible. The crisscrossing currents of the mind-power movement in the first half of the twentieth century produced collaborations among a wide range of spiritual travelers, who traversed the metaphysical landscape with a passion for personal development and self-reinvention.

DOES IT WORK?

If one considers Neville's philosophy, what emerges seems almost too good to be true: Believe that you already possess your goal, and so you will. "Man moves in a world that is nothing more or less than his consciousness objectified," he concluded. If that's true, one might ask, why has this principle been discovered by so relatively few?

In a little-known book from 1946, the occult philosopher Israel Regardie took measure of the burgeoning creative-mind movements, including Unity, Christian Science, and Science of Mind. Regardie paid special attention to the case of Neville, whose teaching, he felt, reflected both the hopes and pitfalls of New Thought philosophy. Regardie believed that Neville possessed profound and truthful ideas; yet he felt these ideas were proffered without sufficient attention to training or practice. Could the everyday person really control his thoughts and moods in the way Neville prescribed? In *The Romance of Metaphysics*, Regardie wrote:

> Neville's method is sound enough. But the difficulty is that few people are able to muster up this emotional exaltation or this intellectual concentration which are the royal approaches to the citadel of the Unconscious. As

a result of this definite lack of training or technique, the mind wanders
all over the place, and a thousand and
one things totally unrelated to 'I AM'
are ever before their attention.

Neville offered his listeners and read-
ers simple meditative techniques, such as
using the practice of visualization before
going to sleep, or the repeat reenactment of
a small, idealized imaginal drama symbol-
izing one's success, like receiving an award
or a congratulatory handshake. But Regardie reasoned that, as a dancer and actor,
Neville possessed a unique control over his
mind and body, which his audience did not
share: "Neville knows the art of relaxation

instinctively. He is a dancer, and a dancer must, of necessity, relax. Hence I believe he does not fully and consciously realize that the average person in his audience does not know the mechanism of relaxation, does know how to 'let go.'

"Of all the metaphysical systems with which I am acquainted," Regardie concluded, "Neville's is the most evidently magical. But being the most magical, it requires for that very reason, a systematized training on the part of those who would approach and enter its portals." Absent this training, Regardie wrote, "His system is in reality strictly personal." It may work for him, the journalist suspected, but not others.

LIVING IN THE
MATERIAL WORLD

Is Regardie's a fair criticism? Certainly testimony exists to the contrary. In his 1961 book *The Law and the Promise* Neville supplied a plethora of letters from people who said they achieved success using his methods. As one reads these passages, however, another impression emerges. Student after student is concerned with ardently material goals: a new house, a new car, a new suit, cash in the pocket. But this was not Neville's ultimate aim.

In a lecture from 1967, Neville drew an intriguing contrast:

> What would be good for you? Tell me, because in the end every conflict will resolve itself as the world is simply mirroring the being you are assuming that you are. One day you will be so saturated with wealth, so saturated with power in the world of Caesar, you will turn your back on it all and go in search of the word of God . . . I do believe that one must completely saturate himself with the things of Caesar before he is hungry for the word of God.

This passage sounds a note that resonates through various esoteric traditions: One cannot renounce what one has not attained. To move beyond the material world, or its wealth, one must know that wealth. But to Neville—and this became the cornerstone of his philosophy—material attainment was merely a step toward the realization of a much greater and ultimate truth.

In the last twelve years of his life, the teacher took his philosophy in a radically new direction—one that cost him some of his popularity on the positive-thinking circuit. Neville told of a jarring mystical experience he had in 1959 in which he was reborn as a child from within his skull, which opened as a womb. (In the Bible, *Golgotha* translates as skull). In a complex interweaving of Scripture and personal experience, Neville told of 'the Promise': that each of us is Christ waiting to be liberated through metaphysical rebirth; this is the true symbolic meaning of the crucifixion in which God became man so that man could one day know himself as God. Our imagination, Neville taught, is the God-seed. He saw literal and final truth in Psalm 82:6, "Ye are gods."

Neville's lecture audiences, however, seemed to prefer the earlier message of affirmative-mind success or what he called "Imaginism." Many listeners, the mystic lamented, "are not at all interested in its framework of faith, a faith leading to the fulfillment of God's promise," as experienced in his vision of rebirth. Audiences drifted away. Urged by his speaking agent to abandon this theme, "or you'll have no audience at all," a student recalled Neville replying, "Then I'll tell it to the bare walls."

When the teacher died of heart failure at his West Hollywood home on October 1, 1972, his passing was marked only by a short obituary in the *Los Angeles Times* and a hastily arranged memorial service. The Age of Aquarius, it seemed, had limited interest in this silver-haired seer who spoke of the human imagination as God.

RESURRECTION

In the early twenty-first century Neville's name would seem to be a relic. But the mystical philosopher has instead experienced a renaissance of attention.

Neville's work is extolled by some of today's bestselling New Age writers, such as Wayne Dyer and Rhonda Byrne. As a result, his books have ridden a new wave of popularity. What's more, Neville's message, perhaps more than that of any other New Thought writer, has prefigured and coalesced with current debates in quantum physics.

Physics journals today routinely discuss what is called the 'quantum measurement problem.' Many people have heard of some version of it. In essence, more than eighty years of laboratory experiments show that atomic-scale particles appear in a given place only when a measurement is made. Quantum theory holds that *no measurement means no precise and localized object*, at least on the atomic scale.

In a challenge to our deepest conceptions of reality, quantum data shows that a subatomic particle literally occupies an infinite number of places (a state called 'superposition') until observation manifests it in one place. In quantum mechanics, an observer's conscious decision to look or not look actually determines what will be there.

For example, quantum experiments

demonstrate that if you project an atom at a pair of boxes *interference patterns prove that the atom was at one point in both boxes*. The particle existed in a wave-state, which means that the location of the particle in space-time is known only probabilistically; it has no properties in this state, just potentialities. The wave became localized in one box only *after* someone looked. Neville described man's power of creation similarly: Thought, he said, does not so much manifest the outcome as *select* it from an infinite universe of already-existing possibilities.

Quantum theory grows still closer to Neville's outlook when dealing with the thought experiment called "Schrödinger's cat." In 1935 the physicist Erwin Schrödinger sought to impel his colleagues to deal with the logical conclusions of their own data—through a purposely absurdist thought experiment. A version goes like this:

A cat is placed into one of a pair of boxes. Along with the cat is what Schrödinger called a "diabolical device." The device, if exposed to an atom, releases a deadly poison. An observer then fires an atom at the boxes. The observer subsequently uses some form of measurement to check on which box the atom is in: the empty one, or the one with the cat and the poisoning device. When the observer goes to check, the wave function of the atom—i.e., the state in which it exists in both boxes—collapses into a particle function—i.e., the state in which it is localized to one box. Once the observer takes his measurement, convention says that the cat will be discovered to be dead or alive. But Schrödinger reasoned that quantum physics describes an outcome in which the cat is *both* dead and alive. This is because the atom, in its wave function, was, at one time, in either box, and either outcome is real.

Neville likewise taught that the mind creates multiple and coexistent realities. Everything already exists in potential, he said, and through our thoughts and feelings we select which outcome we ultimately experience. Indeed, Neville saw man as some quantum theorists see the observer taking measurements in the particle lab, effectively determining where a subatomic particle will actually appear as a localized object. Moreover, Neville wrote that everything and everyone that we experience is rooted in us, as we are ultimately rooted in God. Man exists in an infinite cosmic interweaving of endless dreams of reality—until the ultimate realization of one's identity as Christ.

In an almost prophetic observation in 1948, he told listeners: "Scientists will one day explain why there is a serial universe. But in practice, how you use this serial universe to change the future is more important." More than any other spiritual teacher, Neville created a mystical correlate to quantum physics.

* * *

During his lifetime, Neville never achieved the fame or reputation of his better-known contemporaries, such as Ernest Holmes and Joseph Murphy. Some of his more radical theories cost him segments of his audience. But it was his intellectual bravery, and the elegant congruity of his ideas, that has resulted in his recognition today as one of modern spirituality's most pioneering and foresightful theorists.

This self-taught, unfettered journeyer into the cosmic is likely to emerge as the positive-mind movement's most enduring voice.

A PEN Award–winning historian, **Mitch Horowitz** is the author of *Occult America* and *One Simple Idea*, a history and analysis of the positive-mind movement. He has written on alternative spirituality for *The New York Times, The Washington Post*, and *The Wall Street Journal*. Vice president and executive editor at TarcherPerigee, Mitch is also the voice of popular audio books, including *Alcoholics Anonymous*. Visit him at MitchHorowitz.com.

ABOUT THE AUTHOR

Born to an English family in Barbados, **Neville Goddard** (1905–1972) moved to New York City at age seventeen to study theater. In 1932, he abandoned his work as a dancer and actor to fully devote himself to his career as a metaphysical writer and lecturer. Using the solitary pen name Neville, he became one of the twentieth century's most original and charismatic purveyors of the philosophy generally called New Thought. Neville wrote more than ten books and was a popular speaker on metaphysical themes from the late 1930s until his death. Possessed of a self-educated and eclectic intellect, Neville exerted an influence on a wide range of spiritual thinkers and writers, from Joseph Murphy to Carlos Castaneda. The impact of his ideas continues to be felt in some of today's bestselling works of practical spirituality.